AL•LEONARD

ro vocal
BETTER THAN KARAOKE!

NGBOOK & SOUND-ALIKE CD
TH UNIQUE *PITCH-CHANGER*™

michael bublé crazy

selections from

VOLUME 56

ISBN 978-1-4234-9677-9

HAL•LEONARD®
CORPORATION

7777 W. BLUEMOUND RD. P.O. BOX 13819 MILWAUKEE, WI 53213

lé **crazy love** MB

Visit Hal Leonard Online at
www.halleonard.com

michael bublé selections from crazy love

Cry Me a River

Words and Music by Arthur Hamilton

Intro
Slowly

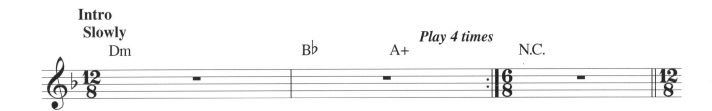

Verse

Now _____ you _____ say you're lone - ly,

you cry _____ the whole night through. _____ Well, you

can cry _____ me a riv - er, _____ cry _____ me a riv - er.

I _____ cried a riv - er o - ver you. _____

4

Verse

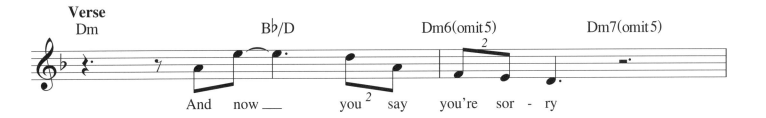

And now ___ you say you're sor - ry

for ___ be - in' so ___ un - true. Well, you

can cry ___ me a riv - er, cry ___ me a riv - er,

'cause I cried a riv - er o - ver you. ___

Bridge

You drove me ___ near - ly out of my head,

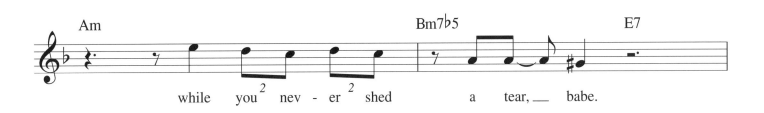

while you nev - er shed a tear, ___ babe.

Re - mem - ber, ___ I re - mem - ber all ___ that you said. ___

You told me love was too ple - be - ian,

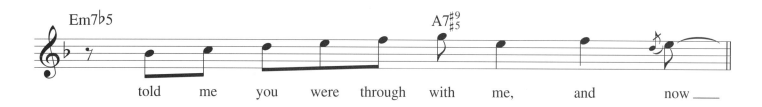

told me you were through with me, and now ___

Verse

___ you say you love me. _____

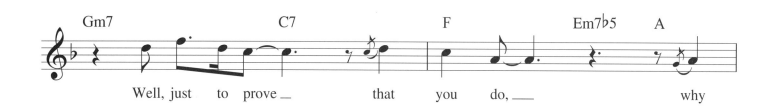

Well, just to prove ___ that you do, ___ why

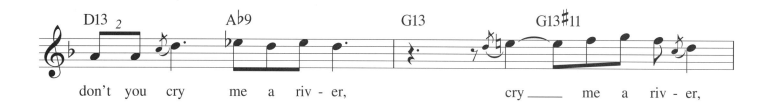

don't you cry me a riv - er, cry _____ me a riv - er,

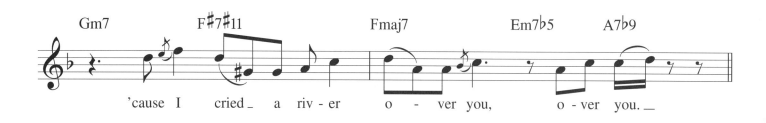

'cause I cried _ a riv - er o - ver you, o - ver you. __

Interlude

You say you love me, but you lied. _____

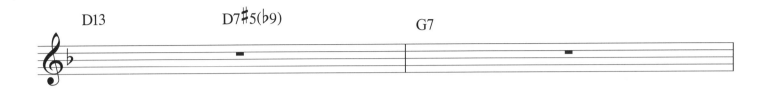

Verse

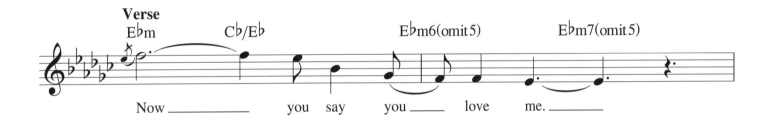

Now _____ you say you _____ love me. _____

Well, just to prove ___ that you do, _____ come on and _

___ cry _____ me a riv - er, whoa, _ cry _____ me a riv - er.

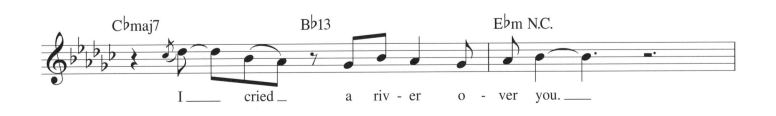

I ___ cried _ a riv - er o - ver you. _____

I _____ cried _____ a riv - er _____

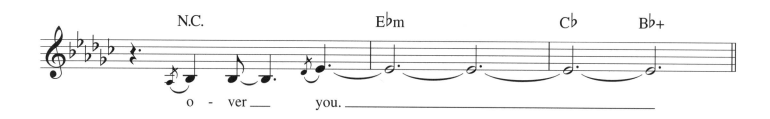

o - ver _____ you. _____

Outro

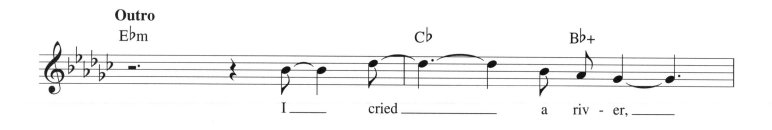

I _____ cried _____ a riv - er, _____

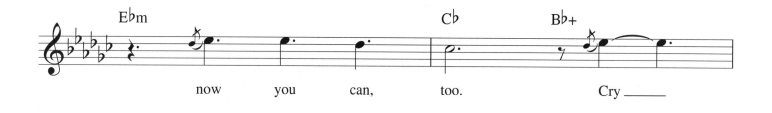

now you can, too. Cry _____

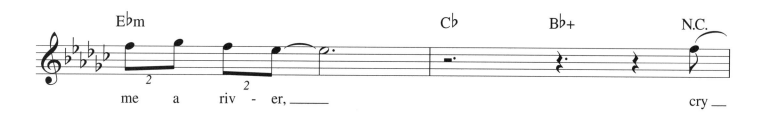

me a riv - er, _____ cry _____

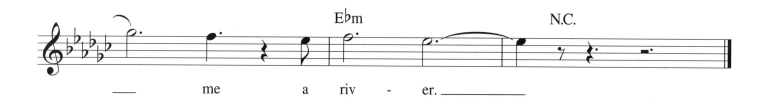

_____ me a riv - er. _____

All of Me

Words and Music by Seymour Simons and Gerald Marks

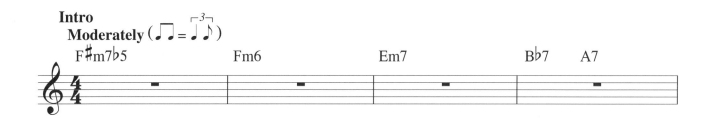

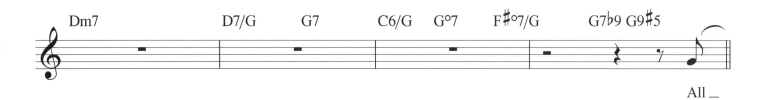

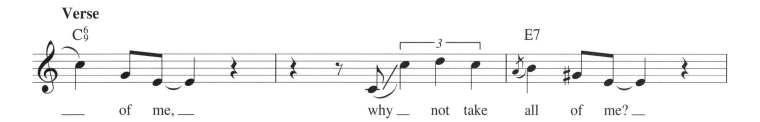

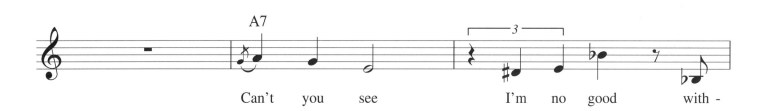

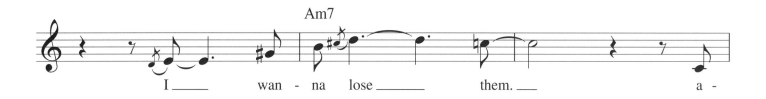

Take my __ arms, _____ I'll _____ nev-er use _____ them. _

Verse

Your good - byes, __ they __ left me

with eyes that cry. __ a - How can I __

__ get a - long __ with - out __ you. __

You _____ took the part _____ that once was my _

__ heart, so __ why not a - take all __ of me? _

Interlude

Let's go, boys, let's go.

Georgia on My Mind

Words by Stuart Gorrell
Music by Hoagy Carmichael

Intro
Ballad

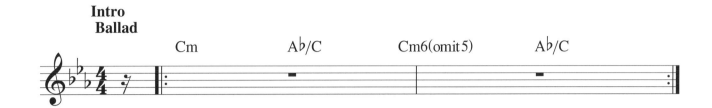

Verse

Geor - gia, ___   Geor - gia,

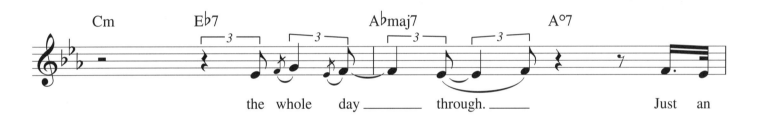

the whole day ___ through. ___   Just an

old sweet ___ song ___   keeps that Geor - gia on ___

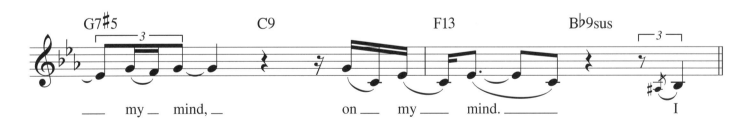

___ my ___ mind, ___   on ___ my ___ mind. ___   I

Verse

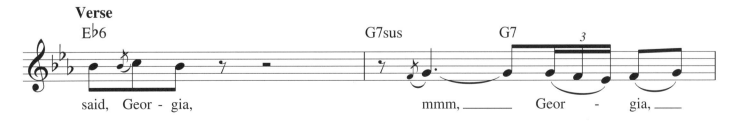

said, Geor - gia,   mmm, ___ Geor - gia, ___

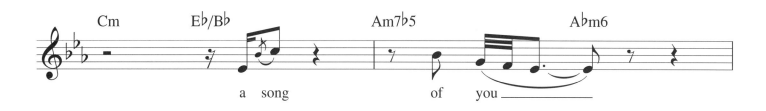

a song of you

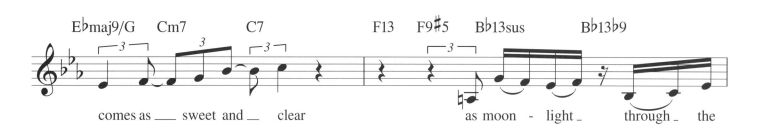

comes as ___ sweet and ___ clear as moon - light ___ through ___ the

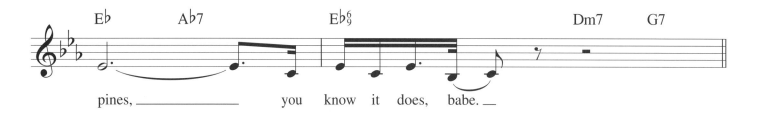

pines, _____ you know it does, babe. ___

Bridge

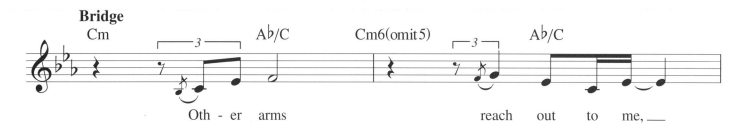

Oth - er arms reach out to me, ___

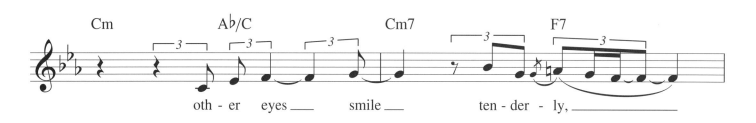

oth - er eyes ___ smile ___ ten - der - ly, _____

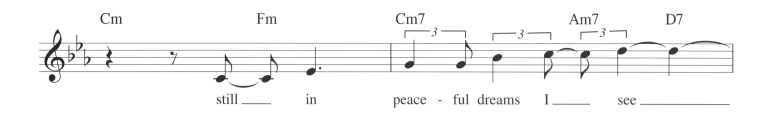

still ___ in peace - ful dreams I ___ see _____

___ the road ___ leads back to you. ___ Oh, _____ I,

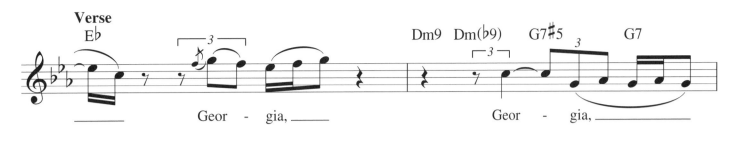

Verse

Geor - gia, _____ Geor - gia, _____

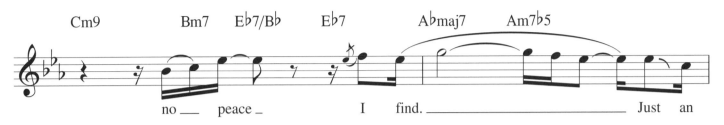

no _____ peace _____ I find. _____ Just an

old _____ sweet song, _____ old _____ sweet song _____ keeps Geor-gia on _____

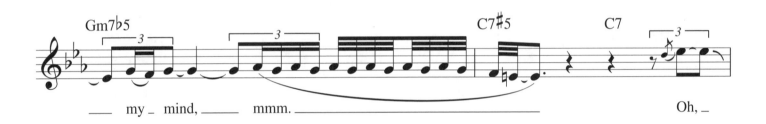

_____ my _____ mind, _____ mmm. Oh, _____

just an old _____ sweet song _____ keeps Geor - gia _____

Outro

on my _____ mind. _____

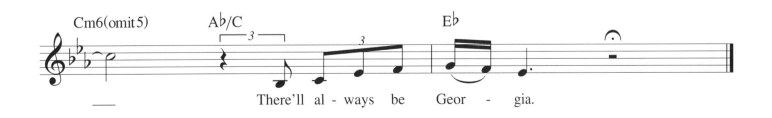

There'll al - ways be Geor - gia.

Crazy Love

Words and Music by Van Morrison

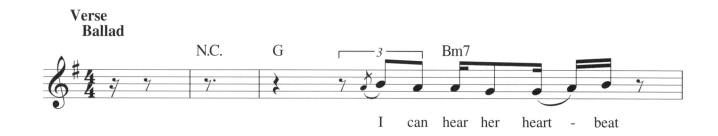

Verse
Ballad

I can hear her heart - beat

for a thou - sand miles, _____ and the heav - ens o - pen up

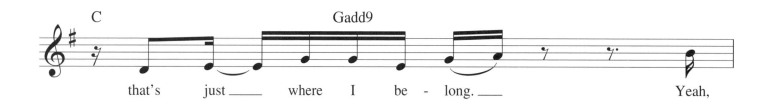

ev - 'ry time she smiles. _____ And when I come to her,

that's just _____ where I be - long. _____ Yeah,

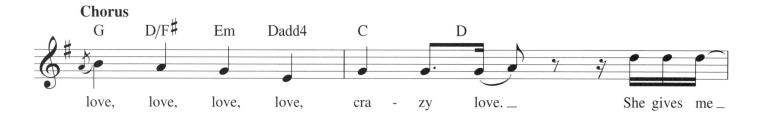

I'm run - nin' to ___ her like a riv - er's song. ___ She give me

Chorus

love, love, love, love, cra - zy love. ___ She gives me ___

cra - zy love. ___ She give me ___ love, _ love, love, love,

cra - zy ___ love. ___ Mmm, _____

cra - zy love. _ She gives me ___ love, _ love, love, love,

cra - zy ___ love. ___ Mmm, _____

Interlude

mmm... _____

Bridge

Yes, I ___ need ___ her ___ in the day - time, ___ oh, ___

___ but I ___ need her in the night. _____

Yes, I wan - na ___ throw my arms a - round ___ her, ___

kiss her, hug, ___ kiss her, ___ hug ___ her tight.

Verse

And when I'm re - turn - in'

from so far a - way, ___ she give me ___ some sweet ___ lov - in',

bright - en up my day. _ Yes, it makes ___ me right - eous, ___

19

it makes __ me feel whole, __ and it makes __ me mel - low

Chorus

down to my soul. __ She gives me love, love, love, love,

cra - zy love. __ She gives me __ love, __ love, love, love, __

cra - zy __ love. __ She gives me __ love, __

uh - huh. I need a - love, love, love, love, __

Outro

cra - zy __ love. __ Cra - zy __ love. __

Cra - zy __ love. __ Cra - zy __ love.

Haven't Met You Yet

Words and Music by Michael Buble, Alan Chang and Amy Foster

Intro

Verse

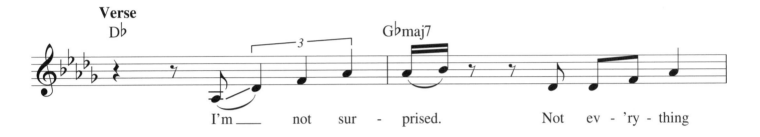

I'm ___ not sur - prised. Not ev - 'ry - thing

lasts. ___ I've bro - ken my heart ___ so man - y times, ___ I stopped

keep - in' ___ track. Talk my - self in, I talk my - self

out. ___ I get all worked up, then I ___ let my - self

Pre-Chorus

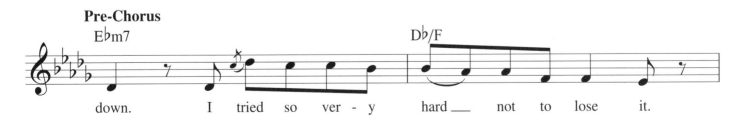

down. I tried so ver - y hard ___ not to lose it.

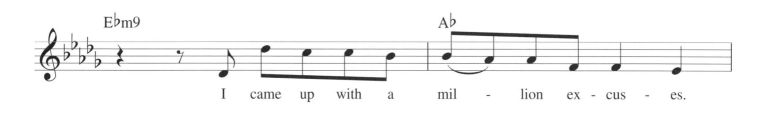

I came up with a mil - lion ex - cus - es.

I thought I'd ___ thought of ev - 'ry pos - si - bil - i - ty. ___

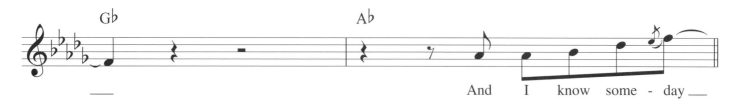

___ And I know some - day ___

Chorus

___ that it - 'll all ___ turn out. a - You'll make me work ___

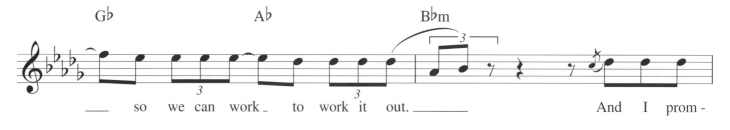

___ so we can work ___ to work it out. ___ And I prom -

ise you, kid, ___ that I'll give ___ so much more ___ than I get.

Interlude

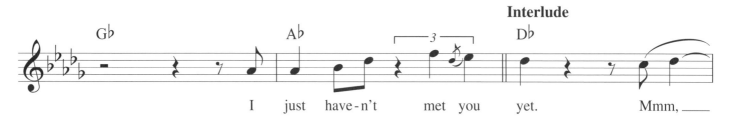

I just have - n't met you yet. Mmm, ___

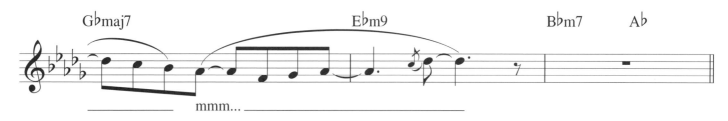

_____ mmm... _____

22

Chorus

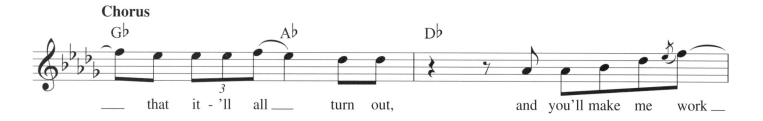

that it - 'll all turn out, and you'll make me work

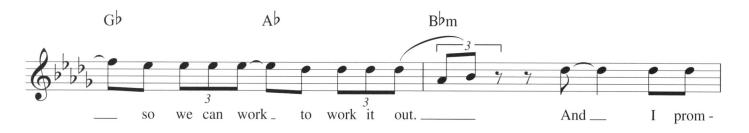

so we can work to work it out. And I prom -

ise you, kid, I'll give so much more than I get.

Bridge

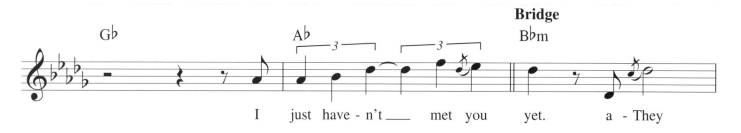

I just have - n't met you yet. a - They

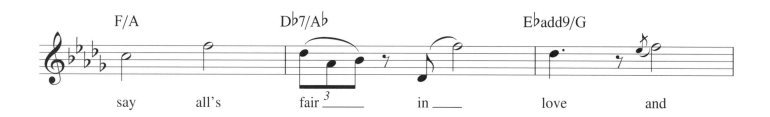

say all's fair in love and

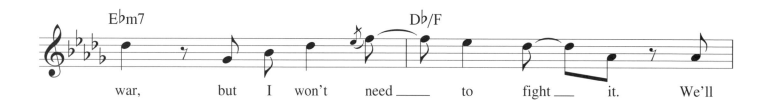

war, but I won't need to fight it. We'll

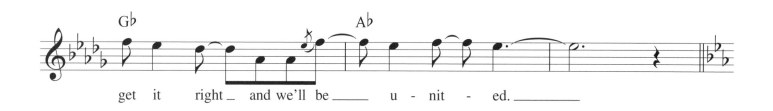

get it right and we'll be u - nit - ed.

Interlude

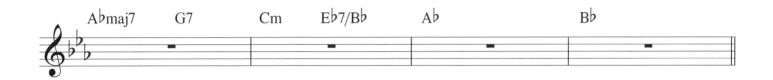

Pre-Chorus

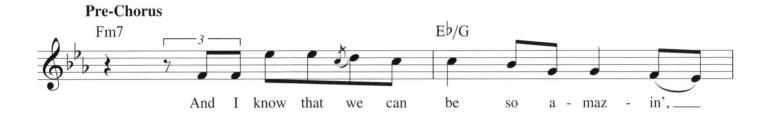

And I know that we can be so a - maz - in', ___

and be - in' in ___ your life is gon - na change ___ me. ___

And now I can ___ see ev - 'ry ___ sin - gle pos -

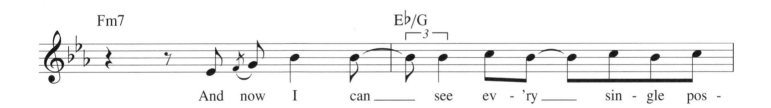

si - bil - i - ty, mmm. _____

Chorus

And some - day I know it - 'll all ___ turn

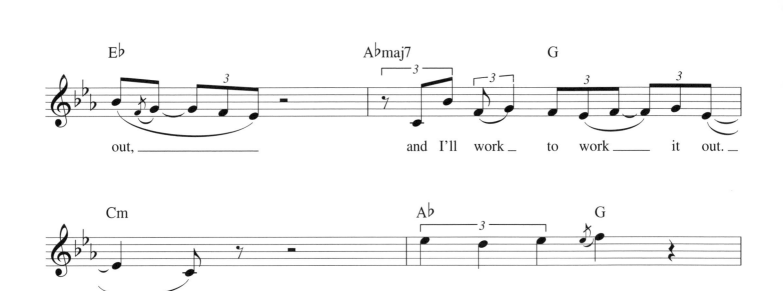

out, _____ and I'll work _ to work _____ it out. _

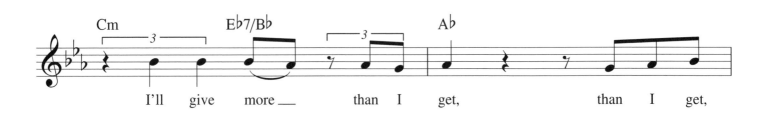

_____ Prom - ise you, kid,

I'll give more __ than I get, than I get,

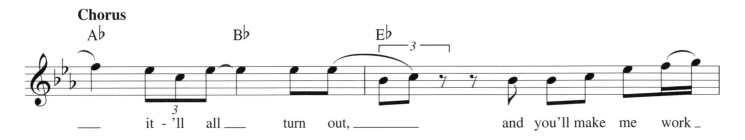

than I get, than I get. Oh, ___ you know __

Chorus

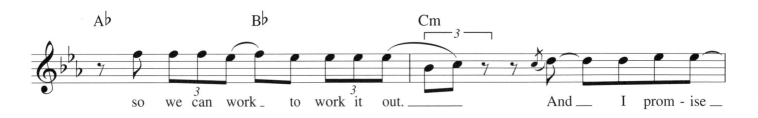

__ it - 'll all __ turn out, _____ and you'll make me work _

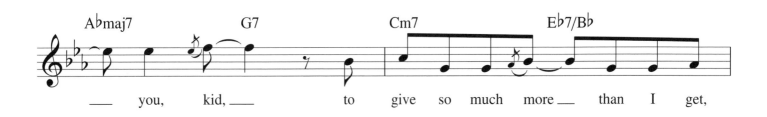

so we can work _ to work it out. _____ And __ I prom - ise __

__ you, kid, __ to give so much more __ than I get,

26

yeah. ___ I just have-n't ___ met you yet.

I just a-have-n't met you ___

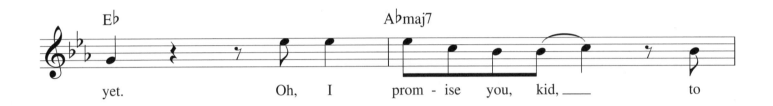

yet. Oh, I prom-ise you, kid, ___ to

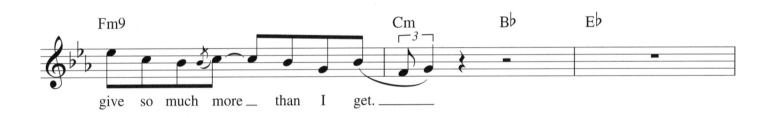

give so much more __ than I get. _____

I just have-n't ___ met ___ you ___

yet. Ja, doi, ___ day, _____ ay, _____ yeah. ___ I

just have-n't met you ___ yet.

All I Do Is Dream of You

Words by Arthur Freed
Music by Nacio Herb Brown

Intro

Chorus

All I do is dream _____ of you _____ the whole _____

_____ night through. _____ With the dawn, I _____

_____ still go on dream - in' of you. _____ You're _____

_____ ev - 'ry thought, you're ev - 'ry - thing, _____ you're

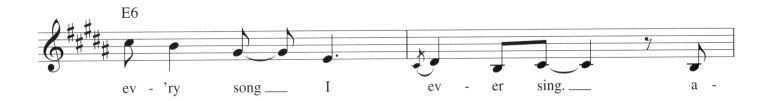

ev - 'ry song ___ I ev - er sing. ___ a -

Sum - mer, ___ a - win - ter, ___ a -

zat, dote, dote -'n'- ba - ba, da - da - da - za - za, in spring. ___ And ___

Chorus

___ were there more ___ than ___ twen - ty - four ___ hours ___

___ in a day, that'd be spent in ___

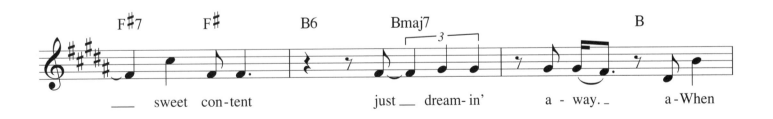

___ sweet con - tent just ___ dream - in' a - way. ___ a - When

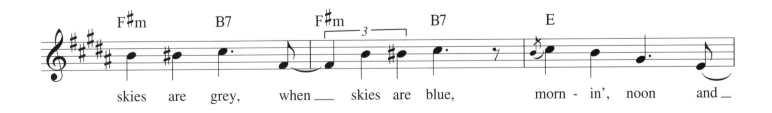

skies are grey, when ___ skies are blue, morn - in', noon and ___

Em   B

__ night - time, __ too,   all   I   do   the

F#7   B   N.C.   G13

whole day   through __ is   dream   of   you.

Interlude

C6   C#°7   Dm7   G7   Dm7   G7

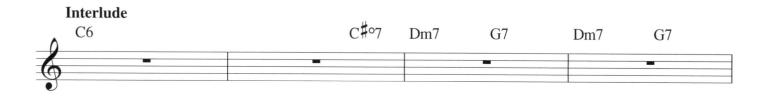

Dm7   G7   Dm7   G7   C

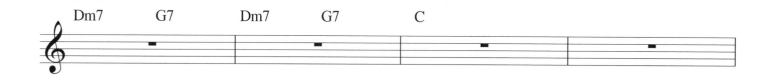

Gm7   C7   Gm7   C7   Fmaj7   F6

When __ skies   are   grey,   e - ven __ when they're

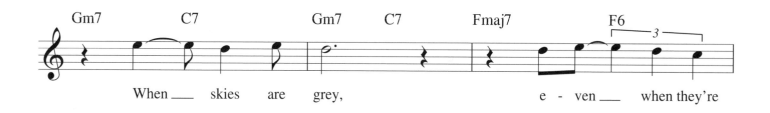

Fm6   D7   D7/C   Bm7   Bbmaj9   Am11   Ab7#11b9   G13

blue...

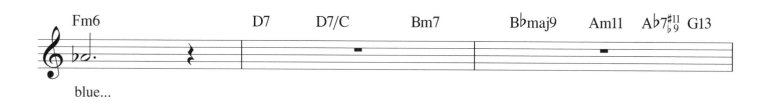

Gb13   F6   Bb/E   C6/G   Db6/G   D6/G   B6   C6   Db6

And __

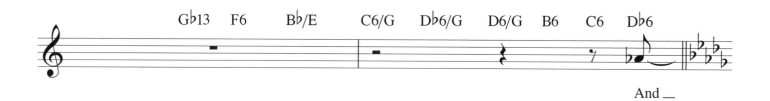

Chorus

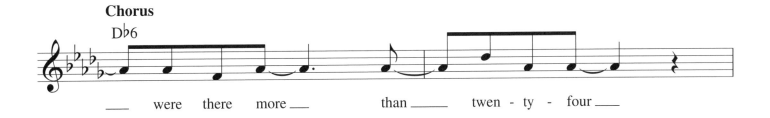

_____ were there more _____ than _____ twen - ty - four _____

ho - urs in a day, _____ oh, that'd be spent _ in _

_____ sweet con - tent dream - in' a - way. _____ a -When

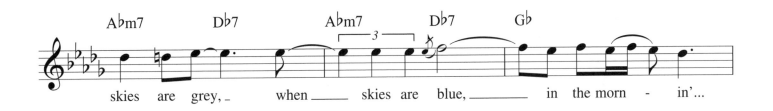

skies are grey, _ when _____ skies are blue, _____ in the morn - in'...

Outro

all I do the _____ whole day _ through is dream _____

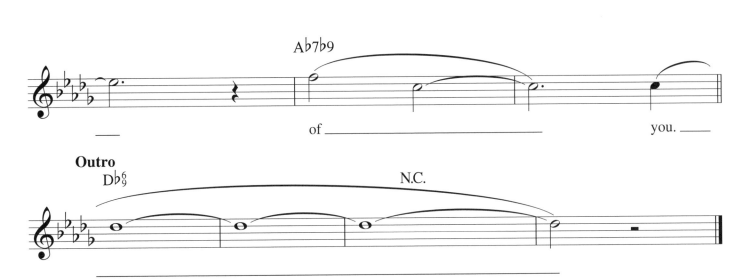

_____ of _____ you. _____

Outro

_____

Hold On

Words and Music by Michael Buble, Alan Chang and Amy Foster

Intro
Ballad

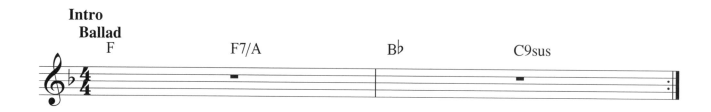

Verse

Did-n't they al-ways _ say _ we were the luck-y ones? _ I guess that we

were once, _ babe, _ we were once. _

But luck will leave you 'cause it is a faith-less friend. And in

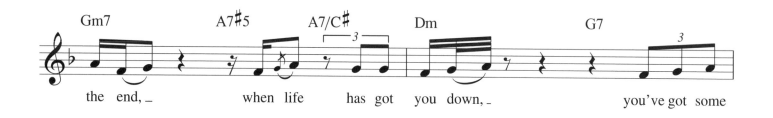

the end, _ when life has got you down, _ you've got some

one here ___ that you can wrap your arms ___ a - round. ___ So, hold ___ on ___

Chorus

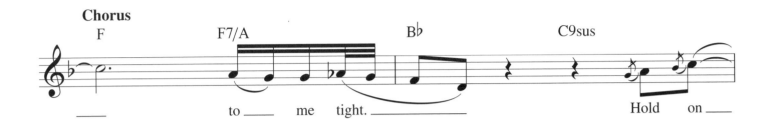

___ to ___ me tight. ___ Hold on ___

___ to me ___ to - night. ___ We are

___ strong-er here ___ to-geth-er than we could ev-er be ___ a-lone, ___ so hold on ___

___ to me, ___ don't you ev-er let me go. ___

Verse

___ There's a thou-sand ways ___ for things to

fall a - part, ___ but it's no one's fault, ___ no, ___ it's not

my fault. ___ And may-be all the plans we made might

not work out, ___ but I have ___ no doubt, ___ e - ven though it's hard to

see. _____ I've got faith for us. I be-lieve in you ___ and me. ___

Chorus

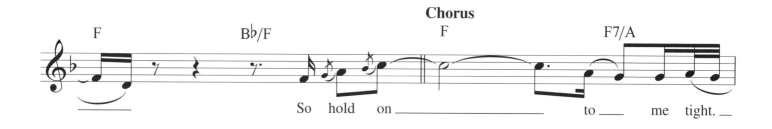

___ So hold on _____ to ___ me tight. ___

___ Hold ___ on, _____ I prom - ise it -'ll be al - right, ___

'cause it's ___ you and me to-geth-er, and ba-by,

all we've got is time, _____ so hold on ___

___ to me, hold on ___ to me to-night. _____

Bridge

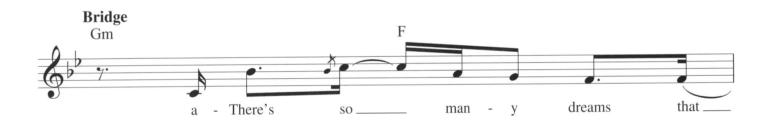

a - There's so _____ man - y dreams that ___

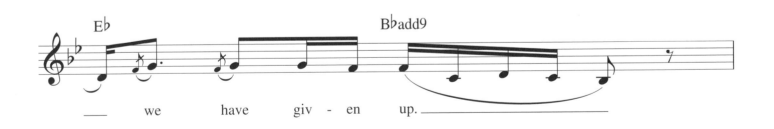

___ we have giv - en up. _____

Take a ___ look at all ___ we've got. _____

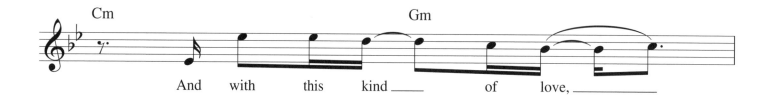

And with this kind _____ of love, _____

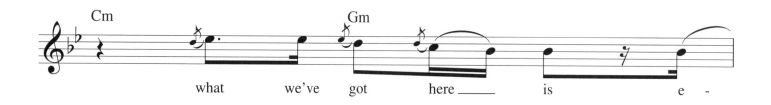

what we've got here _____ is e -

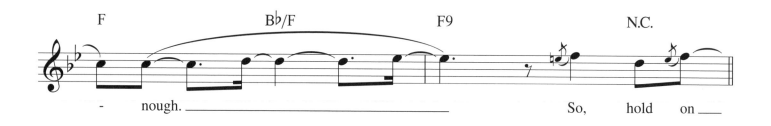

- nough. _____ So, hold on _____

Chorus

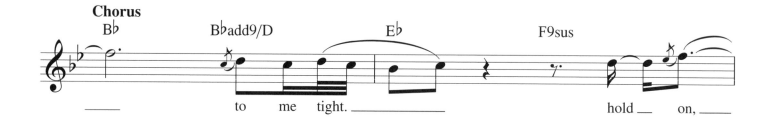

_____ to me tight. _____ hold _____ on, _____

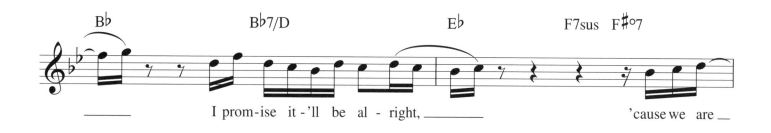

_____ I prom-ise it -'ll be al - right, _____ 'cause we are _____

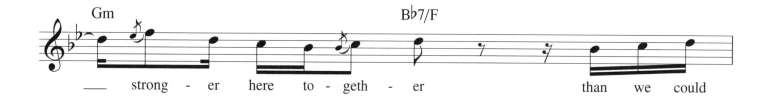

_____ strong - er here to - geth - er than we could

ev - er be a - lone. _____ Just hold on _____

_____ to me, don't you ev - er let _____ me go. _____

Outro

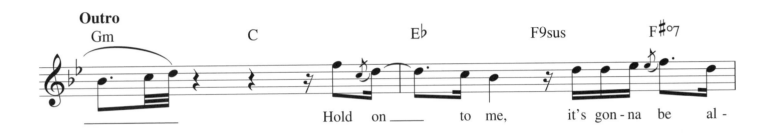

Hold on _____ to me, it's gon - na be al -

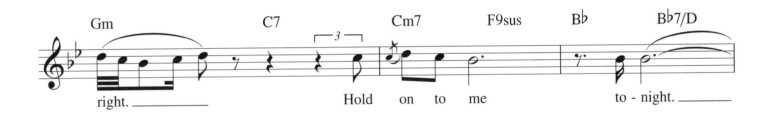

right. _____ Hold on to me to - night. _____

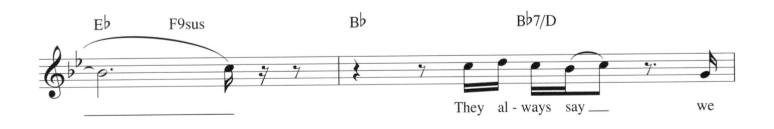

_____ They al - ways say _____ we

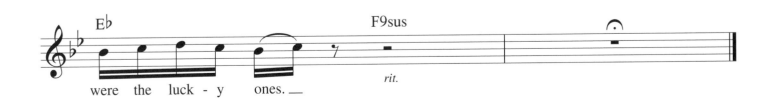

were the luck - y ones. _____ *rit.*

Heartache Tonight

Words and Music by John David Souther, Don Henley, Glenn Frey and Bob Seger

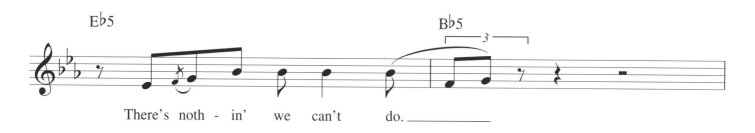

Ev - 'ry-bod - y wants to touch some - bod - y,

if _____ it takes all night. _____

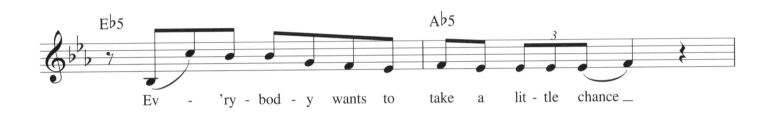

Ev - 'ry - bod - y wants to take a lit - tle chance _____

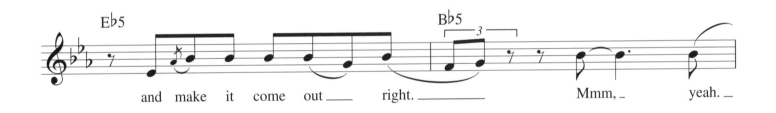

and make it come out _____ right. _____ Mmm, _ yeah. _

Chorus

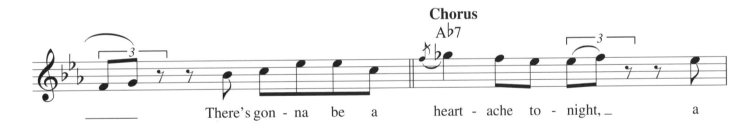

_____ There's gon - na be a heart - ache to - night, _ a

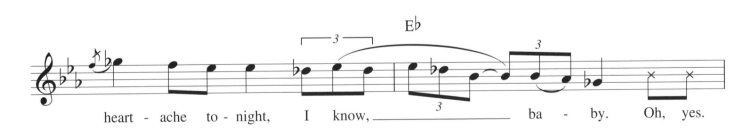

heart - ache to - night, I know, _____ ba - by. Oh, yes.

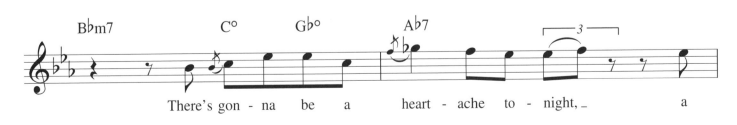

There's gon - na be a heart - ache to - night, _ a

Verse

heart - ache to - night, I know, _____ aw, _____ let's go. _____ a - Some peo - ple like to stay out late, and some folks can't hold out that long, _____ but no - bod - y wants to turn back now. _____ There's too much go - in' on. _____ a - This night is gon - na last for - ev - er, a - last all, _____ last _____ all _____ sum - mer _____ _____ long. a - Some - time be - fore the

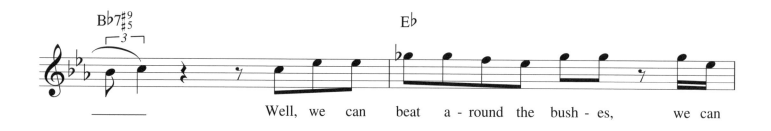

Well, we can beat a - round the bush - es, we can

get down to the bone, we can leave it in the park - ing lot. But

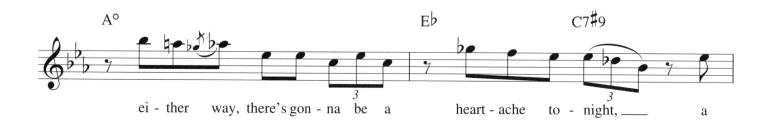

ei - ther way, there's gon - na be a heart - ache to - night, _____ a

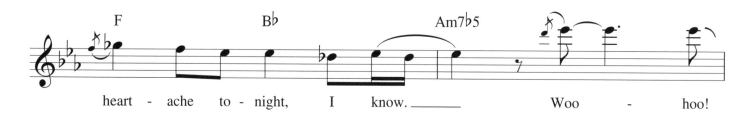

heart - ache to - night, I know. _____ Woo - hoo!

Outro

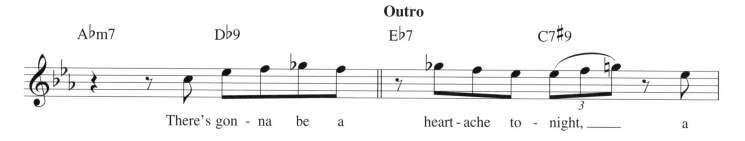

There's gon - na be a heart - ache to - night, _____ a

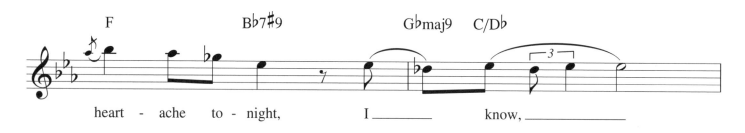

heart - ache to - night, I _____ know, _____

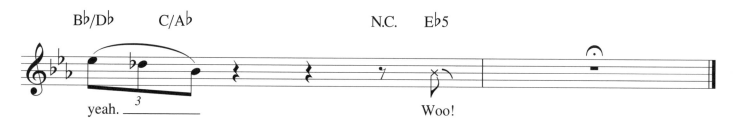

yeah. _____ Woo!

You're Nobody 'Til Somebody Loves You

Words and Music by Russ Morgan, Larry Stock and James Cavanaugh

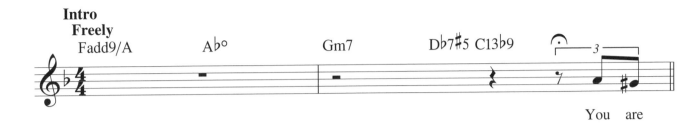

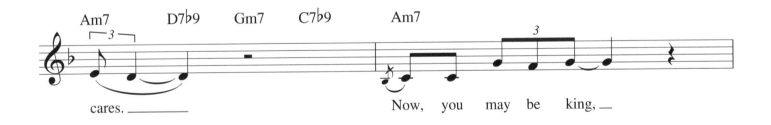

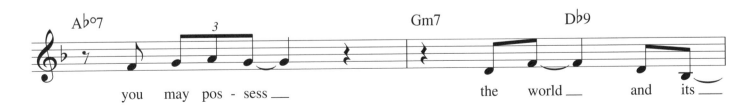

__ gold._ _Gold -'ll nev-er buy _ you hap-pi-ness_

when you're grow - in' old.

Verse
Ballad

_You know the world is the __

__ same, _ a - you'll nev - er change it._

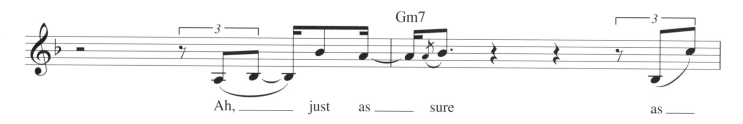

_Ah, _ just as _ sure as __

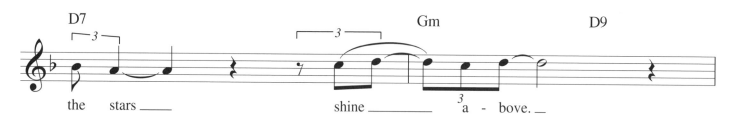

_the stars _ shine _ a - bove. __

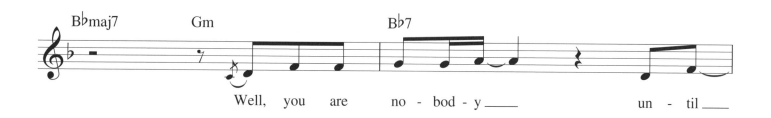

_Well, you are no - bod - y _ un - til __

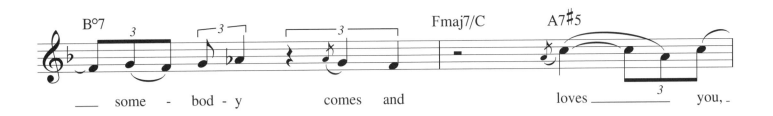

some - bod - y   comes   and   loves _____ you, _

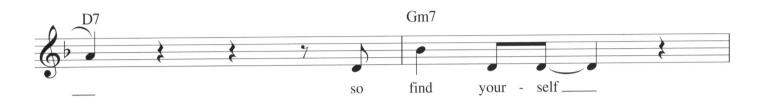

___   so   find   your - self _____

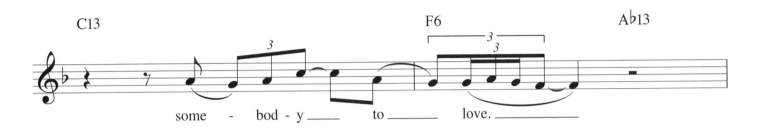

some - bod - y _____ to _____ love. _____

Verse

I   said   the   world, _____   it ___ still   is

the   same, _____   you'll   nev - er   change _____

___   it.   Just _____ as   sure   as _____

___   the   stars _____   shine a - bove.

Good God, ba - by, you ain't no - bod - y un - til

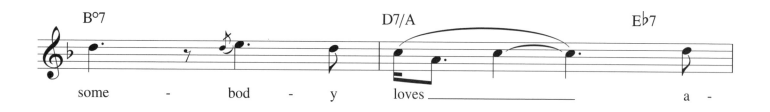

some - bod - y loves a -

you, so find your - self some -

bod - y, I have got me that

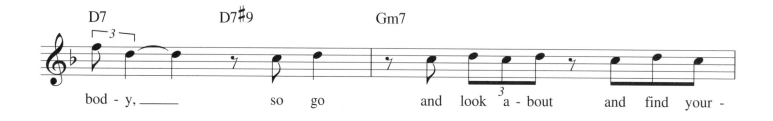

bod - y, so go and look a - bout and find your -

Outro

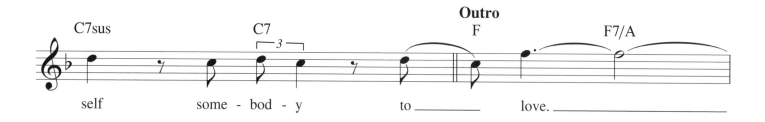

self some - bod - y to love.

At This Moment

Words and Music by Billy Vera

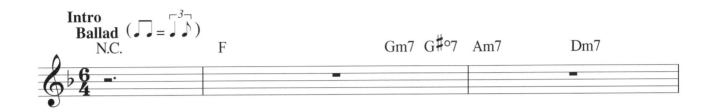

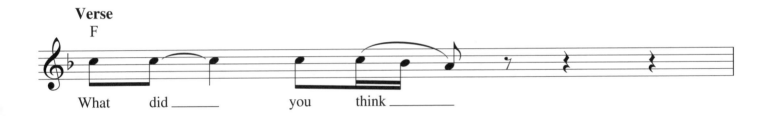

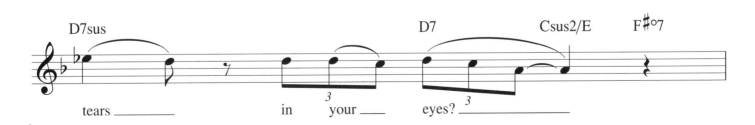

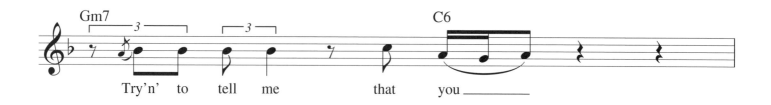

Gm7   C6

Try'n' to tell me   that you _____

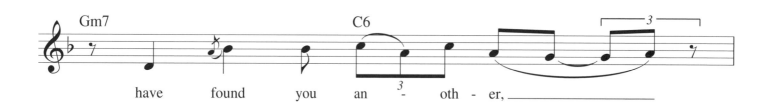

Gm7   C6

have found you an - oth - er, _____

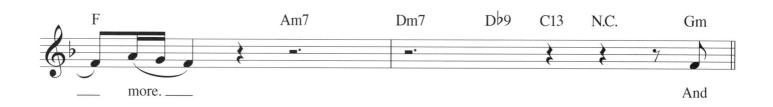

Gm7   C6

and you just don't _____ love me   no _____

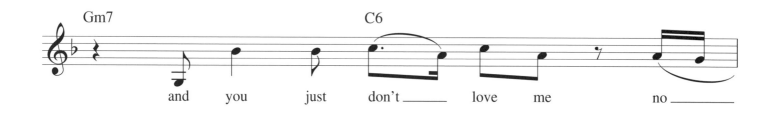

F   Am7   Dm7   D♭9   C13   N.C.   Gm

_____ more. _____   And

Verse

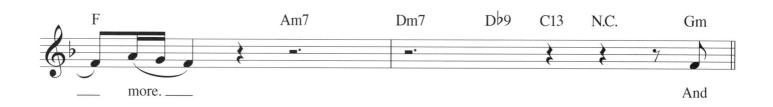

F

what did _____ you think _____

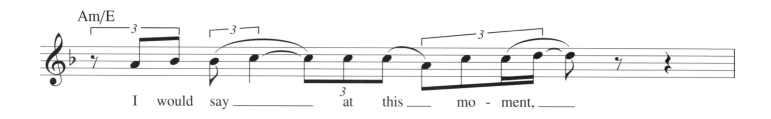

Am/E

I would say _____ at this _____ mo - ment, _____

Cm/E♭

when I'm faced with the knowl - edge _____   that

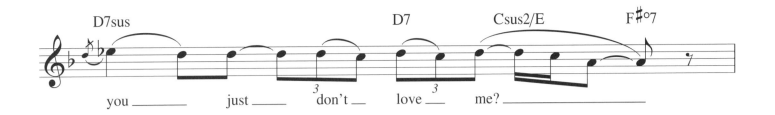

you _____ just _____ don't ___ love ___ me? _____

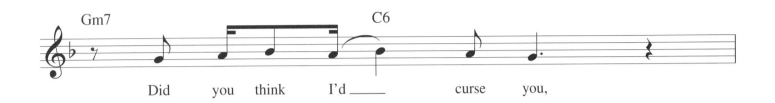

Did you think I'd _____ curse you,

or say things _____ to hurt you,

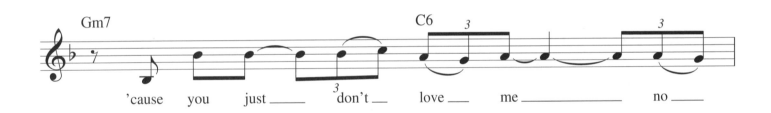

'cause you just _____ don't ___ love ___ me _____ no _____

more? _____ Did

Bridge

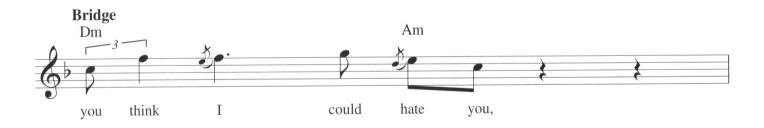

you think I could hate you,

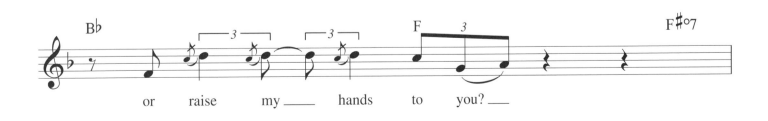

or raise my ___ hands to you? ___

Whoa, ___ come ___ on, you know ___ me too ___ well. ___

___ And how could I hurt you, ___

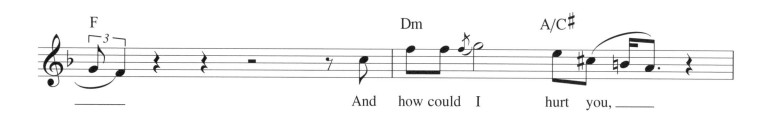

when, dar - lin', I love you,

and you ___ know ___ I would

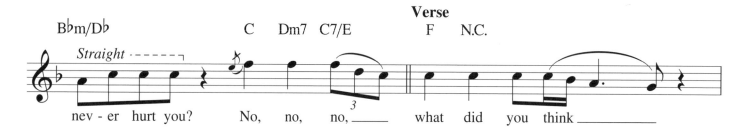

Verse

nev - er hurt you? No, no, no, ___ what did you think ___

I ___ would give at this mo - ment?

If you'd just stay. I'd ___ sub - tract twen -

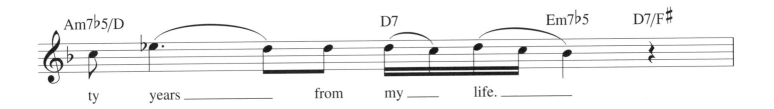

ty   years _____   from   my ____   life. _____

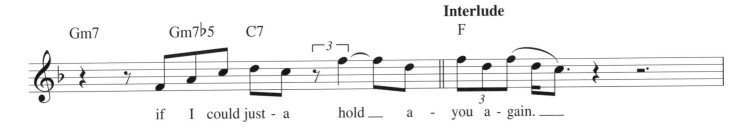

I'd   fall   down   on   my ____   knees,

I'd   kiss   the   ground   that   you   walk   on, _____

Interlude

if   I   could just - a   hold ___   a -   you   a - gain. ____

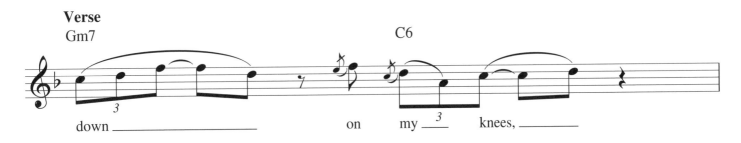

I'd   fall ____

Verse

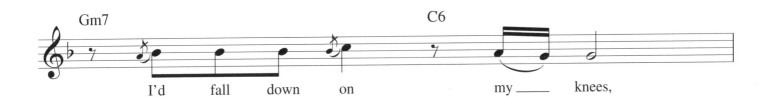

down _____   on   my ___   knees, _____

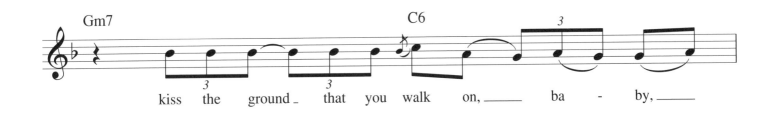

kiss   the   ground ___   that   you   walk   on, _____   ba   -   by, _____

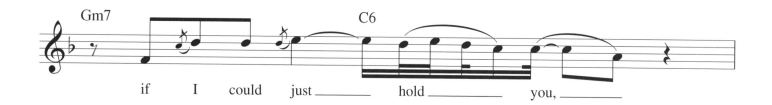

if I could just _____ hold _____ you, _____

mmm, _____ if I could just a - hold you,

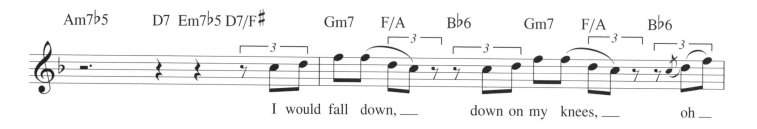

I would fall down, ___ down on my knees, ___ oh ___

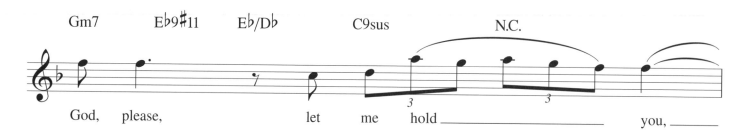

God, please, let me hold _____ you, _____

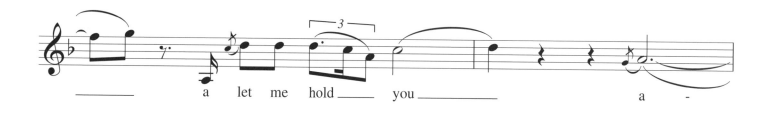

_____ a let me hold _____ you _____ a -

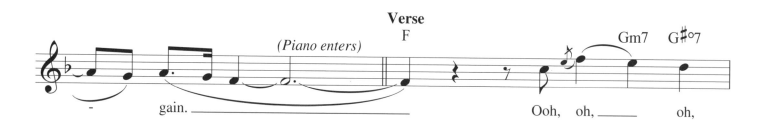

- gain. _____ Ooh, oh, _____ oh,

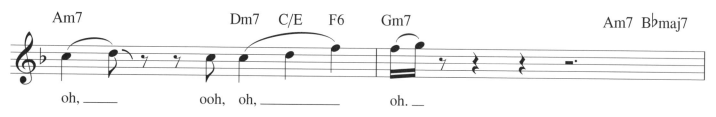

oh, _____ ooh, oh, _____ oh. ___

I'm gon - na miss you, girl, I'm gon - na miss you, girl.

I can see the tears in your eyes, ba - by.

Babe, I'm down, _____ you know I'm down on _____ my knees. _____

Outro

What do you think I would do, ba - by?

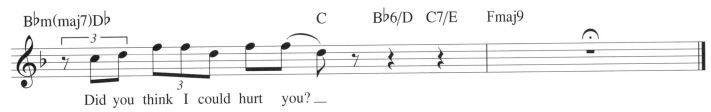

Did you think I could hurt you? __

Pro Vocal® Series
SONGBOOK & SOUND-ALIKE CD
SING 8 GREAT SONGS
WITH A PROFESSIONAL BAND

Whether you're a karaoke singer or an auditioning professional, the Pro Vocal® series is for you! Unlike most karaoke packs, each book in the Pro Vocal Series contains the lyrics, melody, and chord symbols for eight hit songs. The CD contains demos for listening, and separate backing tracks so you can sing along. The CD is playable on any CD player, but it is also enhanced so PC and Mac computer users can adjust the recording to any pitch without changing the tempo! Perfect for home rehearsal, parties, auditions, corporate events, and gigs without a backup band.

WOMEN'S EDITIONS

00740247	**1. Broadway Songs**	$14.95
00740249	**2. Jazz Standards**	$14.95
00740246	**3. Contemporary Hits**	$14.95
00740277	**4. '80s Gold**	$12.95
00740299	**5. Christmas Standards**	$15.95
00740281	**6. Disco Fever**	$12.95
00740279	**7. R&B Super Hits**	$12.95
00740309	**8. Wedding Gems**	$12.95
00740409	**9. Broadway Standards**	$14.95
00740348	**10. Andrew Lloyd Webber**	$14.95
00740344	**11. Disney's Best**	$14.99
00740378	**12. Ella Fitzgerald**	$14.95
00740350	**14. Musicals of Boublil & Schönberg.**	$14.95
00740377	**15. Kelly Clarkson**	$14.95
00740342	**16. Disney Favorites**	$14.99
00740353	**17. Jazz Ballads**	$14.99
00740376	**18. Jazz Vocal Standards**	$16.99
00740375	**20. Hannah Montana**	$16.95
00740354	**21. Jazz Favorites**	$14.99
00740374	**22. Patsy Cline**	$14.95
00740369	**23. Grease**	$14.95
00740367	**25. ABBA**	$14.95
00740365	**26. Movie Songs**	$14.95
00740360	**28. High School Musical 1 & 2**	$14.95
00740363	**29. Torch Songs**	$14.95
00740379	**30. Hairspray**	$14.95
00740380	**31. Top Hits**	$14.95
00740384	**32. Hits of the '70s**	$14.95
00740388	**33. Billie Holiday**	$14.95
00740389	**34. The Sound of Music**	$15.99
00740390	**35. Contemporary Christian**	$14.95
00740392	**36. Wicked**	$15.99
00740393	**37. More Hannah Montana**	$14.95
00740394	**38. Miley Cyrus**	$14.95
00740396	**39. Christmas Hits**	$15.95
00740410	**40. Broadway Classics**	$14.95
00740415	**41. Broadway Favorites**	$14.99
00740416	**42. Great Standards You Can Sing**	$14.99
00740417	**43. Singable Standards**	$14.99
00740418	**44. Favorite Standards**	$14.99
00740419	**45. Sing Broadway**	$14.99
00740420	**46. More Standards**	$14.99
00740421	**47. Timeless Hits**	$14.99
00740422	**48. Easygoing R&B**	$14.99
00740424	**49. Taylor Swift**	$15.99
00740425	**50. From This Moment On**	$14.99
00740426	**51. Great Standards Collection**	$19.99
00740430	**52. Worship Favorites**	$14.99
00740434	**53. Lullabyes**	$14.99
00740438	**54. Lady Gaga**	$14.99

MEN'S EDITIONS

00740248	**1. Broadway Songs**	$14.95
00740250	**2. Jazz Standards**	$14.95
00740251	**3. Contemporary Hits**	$14.99
00740278	**4. '80s Gold**	$12.95
00740298	**5. Christmas Standards**	$15.95
00740280	**6. R&B Super Hits**	$12.95
00740282	**7. Disco Fever**	$12.95
00740310	**8. Wedding Gems**	$12.95
00740411	**9. Broadway Greats**	$14.99
00740333	**10. Elvis Presley – Volume 1**	$14.95
00740349	**11. Andrew Lloyd Webber**	$14.95
00740345	**12. Disney's Best**	$14.95
00740347	**13. Frank Sinatra Classics**	$14.95
00740334	**14. Lennon & McCartney**	$14.95
00740335	**16. Elvis Presley – Volume 2**	$14.99
00740343	**17. Disney Favorites**	$14.99
00740351	**18. Musicals of Boublil & Schönberg.**	$14.95
00740346	**20. Frank Sinatra Standards**	$14.95
00740358	**22. Great Standards**	$14.99
00740336	**23. Elvis Presley**	$14.99
00740341	**24. Duke Ellington**	$14.99
00740359	**26. Pop Standards**	$14.99
00740362	**27. Michael Bublé**	$14.95
00740364	**29. Torch Songs**	$14.95
00740366	**30. Movie Songs**	$14.95
00740368	**31. Hip Hop Hits**	$14.95
00740370	**32. Grease**	$14.95
00740371	**33. Josh Groban**	$14.95
00740373	**34. Billy Joel**	$14.99
00740381	**35. Hits of the '50s**	$14.95
00740382	**36. Hits of the '60s**	$14.95
00740383	**37. Hits of the '70s**	$14.95
00740385	**38. Motown**	$14.95
00740386	**39. Hank Williams**	$14.95
00740387	**40. Neil Diamond**	$14.95
00740391	**41. Contemporary Christian**	$14.95
00740397	**42. Christmas Hits**	$15.95
00740399	**43. Ray**	$14.95
00740400	**44. The Rat Pack Hits**	$14.99
00740401	**45. Songs in the Style of Nat "King" Cole**	$14.99
00740402	**46. At the Lounge**	$14.95
00740403	**47. The Big Band Singer**	$14.95
00740404	**48. Jazz Cabaret Songs**	$14.99
00740405	**49. Cabaret Songs**	$14.99
00740406	**50. Big Band Standards**	$14.99
00740412	**51. Broadway's Best**	$14.99
00740427	**52. Great Standards Collection**	$19.99
00740431	**53. Worship Favorites**	$14.99
00740435	**54. Barry Manilow**	$14.99
00740436	**55. Lionel Richie**	$14.99
00740439	**56. Michael Bublé – Crazy Love**	$14.99
00740441	**57. Johnny Cash**	$14.99

MIXED EDITIONS

These editions feature songs for both male and female voices.

00740311	**1. Wedding Duets**	$12.95
00740398	**2. Enchanted**	$14.95
00740407	**3. Rent**	$14.95
00740408	**4. Broadway Favorites**	$14.99
00740413	**5. South Pacific**	$15.99
00740414	**6. High School Musical 3**	$14.99
00740429	**7. Christmas Carols**	$14.99
00740437	**8. Glee**	$15.99
00740440	**9. More Songs from Glee**	$19.99

FOR MORE INFORMATION, SEE YOUR LOCAL MUSIC DEALER, OR WRITE TO:

HAL•LEONARD®
CORPORATION
7777 W. BLUEMOUND RD. P.O. BOX 13819 MILWAUKEE, WI 53213

Visit Hal Leonard online at www.halleonard.com

Prices, contents, & availability subject to change without notice.
Disney charaters and artwork © Disney Enterprises, Inc.

0511